EVERYTHING SUPER BOWL

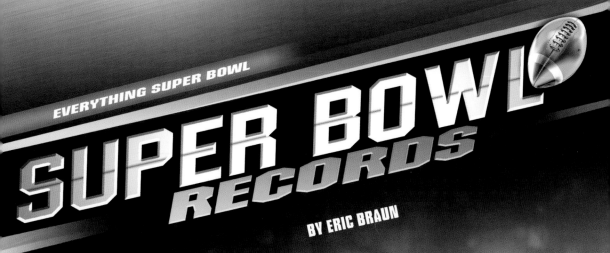

SUPER BOWL
RECORDS

BY ERIC BRAUN

CAPSTONE PRESS
a capstone imprint

Sports Illustrated Kids Everything Super Bowl is published by Capstone Press
1710 Roe Crest Drive, North Mankato, Minnesota 56003.
www.mycapstone.com

Library of Congress Cataloging-in-Publication Data is available on the Library of
Congress website.

ISBN 978-1-5157-2636-4 (library binding)
ISBN 978-1-5157-2640-1 (eBook PDF)

Editorial Credits
Nick Healy, editor; Ted Williams, designer; Eric Gohl, media researcher;
Gene Bentdahl, production specialist

Photo Credits
Getty Images: James Flores, 5, Stringer/George Rose, 18; Newscom: Icon SMI/
Sporting News/Albert Dickson, 11, KRT/Scott Powers, 24; Sports Illustrated:
Al Tielemans, cover (bottom), 12, 25, Andy Hayt, 14, 20, Bill Frakes, 22, Heinz
Kluetmeier, 28, John Biever, 6, John Iacono, cover (top left & top right), 8, 15, Peter
Read Miller, 16, Walter Iooss Jr., 10, 26, 29
Design Elements: Shutterstock

Printed in the United States of America.
009677F16

TABLE OF CONTENTS

THE BIG GAME

The first Super Bowl wasn't even called the Super
Bowl. On January 15, 1967, the Green Bay Packers
defeated the Kansas City Chiefs in "The AFL-NFL World
Championship Game." The game pitted the top teams
from the American Football League and the National
Football League against each other. Held at the Los
Angeles Memorial Coliseum, it didn't even sell out.

Bart Starr, quarterback of the Packers, threw for
250 yards in a winning effort that day. His record for
passing yards in a Super Bowl lasted until the Steelers'
great Terry Bradshaw topped him with 318 passing yards
in Super Bowl XIII.

Today the Super Bowl is one of the most popular
sporting events in the world. Over time, the game has
changed. New stars have emerged, new strategies have
gained popularity, and people have been lucky—or
unlucky. And records have fallen. Today, the record
for passing yards in a Super Bowl is 414 yards, set by
the Rams' Kurt Warner in Super Bowl XXXIV. In time,
someone will surely beat that record, too.

That's the nature of records. They are made to be
broken. But the names and stories that go with those
historic performances will never change. That's what's so
fun about Super Bowl records—the stories.

◄ Bart Starr

AIR SHOW

Kurt Warner ▼

The story of Kurt Warner was already so surprising, it seemed like a fairy tale.

He went undrafted after college and worked in a grocery store for minimum wage. From 1995 to 1997, he played for the Iowa Barnstormers in the Arena Football League. He was finally signed by the St. Louis Rams but only got the chance to play after the starter, Trent Green, suffered an injury that ended his season.

Warner had never started an NFL game before. Would he be up to the task? Fans quickly changed their tune from "Who's that guy?" to "That's our guy!" as Warner threw for 4,353 yards and 41 touchdowns that season. The Rams set an NFL record for points scored in a season with 526. The player who nobody had even heard of a few months earlier was named the league's most valuable player (MVP). And the Rams were on their way to Super Bowl XXXIV, to be played in January 2000.

St. Louis was expected to easily beat the Tennessee Titans, but late in the fourth quarter, Tennessee tied the game at 16. It looked like the high-powered Rams were choking under the pressure. Warner had been battered all game long. He was suffering from brutal rib pain as he jogged out for the team's final drive. Even though his team had only 16 points to show for it, he had passed for a remarkable 341 yards. His next pass was the big one: He connected with wide receiver Isaac Bruce for a 73-yard game-winning score.

Those 73 yards helped deliver a Rams victory. They also gave Warner a total of 414 passing yards for the day—the most ever for a quarterback in a single Super Bowl.

"I guess it is sort of a storybook ending," Warner told reporters after the game. "When you think about where I was and where I am now, it seems pretty incredible."

— TOP THREE SUPER BOWL — PASSING PERFORMANCES

Kurt Warner wasn't finished after that magical season. He returned to the Super Bowl twice more—once with the Rams and once with the Arizona Cardinals—setting the second and third place records for most passing yards in a Super Bowl.

414 yards	Kurt Warner	Rams vs. Titans	XXXIV
377 yards	Kurt Warner	Cardinals vs. Steelers	XLIII
365 yards	Kurt Warner	Rams vs. Patriots	XXXVI

RUNNING WILD

Timmy Smith ▼

— MOST YARDS GAINED, —
SINGLE SUPER BOWL

204	Timmy Smith	Redskins vs. Broncos	Super Bowl XXII
191	Marcus Allen	Raiders vs. Redskins	Super Bowl XVIII
166	John Riggins	Redskins vs. Dolphins	Super Bowl XVII

The big stories going into Super Bowl XXII were about the quarterbacks. John Elway, the charismatic QB for the Denver Broncos, was a huge star. Surely he would put on a big scoring show. The Washington Redskins' Doug Williams was the first African-American quarterback to start a Super Bowl. In 1988 that was news in itself.

Washington running back Timmy Smith was a shy fifth-round pick with few carries in his career. He had been a backup all season. But in a surprise move, coach Joe Gibbs started Smith over aging star George Rogers.

After the first quarter, the game was playing out the way most people expected. Denver was up 10-0, and Washington couldn't seem to get anything going. But the second quarter was a different story.

"Let's get this sucker rolling!" Williams yelled at his teammates in the huddle.

In the second quarter, Williams completed nine passes for 228 yards and four touchdowns. Washington scored 35 unanswered points.

But that wasn't the record-setting performance. Running back Timmy Smith carried five times for 122 yards and one touchdown that quarter alone. In the second half, the Redskins kept handing Smith the ball in an effort to keep the clock ticking. Their burly offensive line tore open holes for him all day, and Smith galloped through them. By the end of the game, he had romped for a Super Bowl-record 204 yards.

GREATS ON THE GROUND

Franco Harris ▼

When Franco Harris was drafted in 1972, the Pittsburgh Steelers had never made the playoffs. That season Harris rushed for more than 1,000 yards and scored 12 touchdowns. The Steelers went to the playoffs for the first time. Two years later Pittsburgh made the Super Bowl.

Pittsburgh was known as a defense-first team. Their physical D overwhelmed the Minnesota Vikings in Super Bowl IX, played in January 1975. On offense the Steelers were fairly one-dimensional: They relied on a fantastic running game led by Harris. He carried the ball 34 times for 158 yards and was named the game's MVP.

— THE IMMACULATE RECEPTION —

In Pittsburgh's first-ever playoff game, Steelers quarterback Terry Bradshaw threw a pass that bounced off a player and looked like an incompletion in the making. The ball had nearly hit the turf when Franco Harris reached down and nabbed it. He ran 42 yards for the winning touchdown, and the play became known as "The Immaculate Reception."

— MOST RUSHING YARDS — GAINED, CAREER

354	Franco Harris	Steelers	4 games
297	Larry Csonka	Dolphins	3 games
289	Emmitt Smith	Cowboys	3 games

Defense remained Pittsburgh's strength as the team went to three more Super Bowls in the 1970s. In Super Bowl X in 1976, Harris gained 82 yards. In Super Bowl XIII in 1979, he tacked on another 68. He gained only 46 yards in Super Bowl XIV in 1980, the last time his Steelers would go to the big game. That effort was enough to give him 354 career rushing yards in the Super Bowl. Nearly 40 years later, his record still stands.

Emmitt Smith ▲

Legendary tough man Larry Csonka went to three Super Bowls with the Miami Dolphins. To cap off the Dolphins' perfect season in 1972, he rushed for 112 yards on 15 carries, helping his team win Super Bowl VII. He finished his career with 297 yards rushing in Super Bowls, good for second all-time.

The back with the third-most rushing yards in Super Bowls is Emmitt Smith. In the 1990s, Smith's Dallas Cowboys went to three Super Bowls, winning them all. They rode Smith's powerful legs all the way. He gained 108 yards in Super Bowl XXVII and 132 yards the following year in XXVIII, for which he was named the game's MVP. He tacked on 49 yards in Super Bowl XXX to bring his career total to 289.

THE LONG RUN

Willie Parker ▲

— LONGEST RUNS FROM SCRIMMAGE —
IN SUPER BOWL HISTORY

75 yards	Willie Parker	Steelers vs. Seahawks	XL (TD)
74 yards	Marcus Allen	Raiders vs. Redskins	XVIII (TD)
58 yards	Tom Matte	Colts vs. Jets	III
58 yards	Timmy Smith	Redskins vs. Broncos	XXII (TD)

Early in the season, Steelers running back Willie Parker had been a backup, playing behind his team's top two rushers. Parker filled in ably when other backs went out with injuries. He was the starter when the Steelers made it to Super Bowl XL, but he was hardly a feared runner.

The Steelers were more of a passing team, led by quarterback Ben Roethlisberger and wideout Hines Ward. But early in the game, the Seattle Seahawks' defense confused Roethlisberger with a variety of different looks. By halftime the Steelers had produced a mere seven points.

Injured running back Jerome Bettis pulled Parker aside to point out something he'd noticed about how the Seahawks' safeties were playing. Parker later recalled, "He said, 'They know you want to hit the home run to the outside.' He told me to go outside in."

Parker's chance came on the second play of the second half—a run off tackle. Steelers guard Alan Faneca made a terrific block to open the hole. Ward laid a great block on cornerback Andre Dyson to help Parker get through the secondary. Parker ran toward the outside, then cut back in. His blazing speed did the rest.

"I took Jerome's advice, and it was absolute daylight," Parker said. With no defender in the same time zone, he dove into the end zone and did a somersault. His 75-yard run is the longest run from scrimmage in Super Bowl history. The Steelers went on to win 21-10.

For 22 years Raiders legend Marcus Allen held the record for longest Super Bowl run. Facing Washington in Super Bowl XVIII, Allen dashed 74 yards for a TD late in the third quarter. The Raiders won, 38-9.

JOE COOL

Great stories and signature victories are two good ways to measure a great quarterback. Sometimes statistics speak volumes. When it comes to Joe Montana, the greatest Super Bowl quarterback of all, one statistic clearly demonstrates his success: passer rating. In four Super Bowls with the San Francisco 49ers, all wins, Montana compiled a 127.8 passer rating.

— HIGHEST SUPER BOWL — PASSER RATING, CAREER
(AT LEAST 40 ATTEMPTS)

127.8	Joe Montana	49ers	4 games
122.8	Jim Plunkett	Raiders	2 games
112.8	Terry Bradshaw	Steelers	4 games

Passer rating is figured using a complex formula that takes into account a player's passing attempts, completions, yards, touchdowns, and interceptions. It's measured on a scale of 0 to 158.3. Any number over 100 is outstanding. Montana's Super Bowl rating is out of sight.

▼ Joe Montana

Oh, Montana had plenty of great stories and signature victories, too. Probably his greatest performance came in Super Bowl XXIV, his fourth. Perhaps hoping to intimidate the 49ers, the Denver Broncos—the league's number-one defense—had publicly promised to hit hard. They wanted to punish the 49ers' offense.

Instead, Montana threw for 297 yards with five touchdowns and no interceptions. San Francisco scored TDs on eight of their first 11 possessions and blew out Denver 55-10. It was the most points ever scored by a team in the Super Bowl and the largest margin of victory.

Broncos defensive coordinator Wade Phillips said, "We tried everything, and nothing worked."

ARM OF A CHAMPION

◀ Tom Brady

— BRADY IN THE BIG GAME —

Super Bowl	Score	Passing Yards
XXXVI	Patriots 20–Rams 17	145
XXXVIII	Patriots 32–Panthers 29	354
XXXIX	Patriots 24–Eagles 21	236
XLII	Giants 17–Patriots 14	266
XLVI	Giants 21–Patriots 17	276
XLIX	Patriots 28–Seahawks 24	328

ere was Tom Brady: an average college quarterback fighting for starts with more talented players. He didn't have great arm strength. He wasn't very quick or mobile. His coach at the University of Michigan preferred those other quarterbacks—the more athletic quarterbacks. So did the fans.

Brady was a backup.

When he got a chance to play, he performed well. But he knew if he wanted to start, he had to improve. So he studied film almost every night. He learned to anticipate when receivers would get open. He began to recognize defenses. Driven by all those doubters, he became smarter. And better.

The next year Brady earned the starting job. He finished his college career by beating Alabama in the Orange Bowl. He tossed four touchdowns in that game to go with 369 passing yards.

Even then, he wasn't seen as a star. The New England Patriots didn't draft him until the sixth round—199th overall. In his rookie season, he played just one game. He watched star quarterback Drew Bledsoe from the bench. But when Bledsoe got injured early in the 2001 season, Brady took over and never looked back. In fact, he led his team to a Super Bowl victory that season.

Brady and the Patriots returned to the Super Bowl five more times, and Brady has racked up more career passing yards in the Super Bowl than anyone in history. And he's not finished yet.

— MOST SUPER BOWL — PASSING YARDS, CAREER

1,605	Tom Brady	Patriots	6 games
1,156	Kurt Warner	Rams/Cardinals	3 games
1,142	Joe Montana	49ers	4 games
1,128	John Elway	Broncos	5 games

SUPER SIX

Steve Young

Some Super Bowls are entertaining, down-to-the-wire thrillers. Not Super Bowl XXIX. That one was a clunker, unless you were a 49ers fan.

Throughout the early 1990s, two teams were clearly better than all the rest: the Dallas Cowboys and the 49ers. But since both teams were in the National Football Conference (NFC), they could never meet in the Super Bowl. Three years in a row, they duked it out to claim the NFC Championship. To many, that was the "real" Super Bowl. The winner went on to demolish whoever won the American Football Conference (AFC).

During the 1980s and 1990s, the NFC won 16 of the 20 Super Bowls. That included 13 straight wins from Super Bowl XIX in 1985 to Super Bowl XXXI in 1997.

18

In Super Bowl XXIX, the AFC produced the San Diego Chargers for the annual sacrifice. In that season's previous meeting between the teams, the 49ers had beaten the Chargers 38-15. In the regular season, the Chargers played their linebackers deeper than usual to prevent big plays. Quarterback Steve Young simply nicked them to death on short pass after short pass. This time, the Chargers decided to play tighter. Bad idea.

Just over one minute into the game, Young hit Jerry Rice for a 44-yard touchdown. It looked so easy that fans seemed to understand one thing: This game was over.

"To be honest," said one Chargers official, "we knew we were in trouble when we lost the coin toss."

Young went on to throw five more touchdowns that day, including two more to Rice. The previous record for Super Bowl TD tosses was held by another 49ers great, Joe Montana. He threw five in Super Bowl XXIV against the Broncos.

The incredible thing is, Young could have thrown even more. His coach, George Seifert, pulled him and the other offensive stars in the fourth quarter.

— MOST INTERCEPTIONS THROWN — IN A SINGLE SUPER BOWL

5	Rich Gannon	Raiders vs. Buccaneers	XXXVII
4	Craig Morton	Broncos vs. Cowboys	XII
4	Jim Kelly	Bills vs. Redskins	XXVI
4	Drew Bledsoe	Patriots vs. Packers	XXXI
4	Kerry Collins	Giants vs. Ravens	XXXV

CATCHING THE BOMBS

There has never been a better wide receiver than Jerry Rice. You won't find too many people who will argue that. He's the G.O.A.T.—the Greatest of All Time—at his position. Some people even say he was the greatest of all time NFL player at *any* position.

◀ **Jerry Rice**

— MOST SUPER BOWL — RECEPTIONS, CAREER

Receptions	Player	Team(s)	Super Bowls
33	Jerry Rice	49ers/Raiders	4 games
27	Andre Reed	Bills	4 games
21	Deion Branch	Patriots	2 games

Over a career spent mostly with the San Francisco 49ers, Rice accumulated more catches than anyone in history: 1,549. He racked up more receiving yards than anyone: 22,895. That's more than 13 miles, or half a marathon—a few yards at a time. One hundred ninety-seven of those catches went for touchdowns, also the best of all time.

But Rice cemented his legacy in Super Bowls. He had plenty of chances to do that cementing, since he played in four of them. In those games, he caught 33 passes for 589 yards and eight touchdowns. All three of those numbers are records.

In Super Bowl XXIII, against the Cincinnati Bengals, Rice caught 11 passes for 215 yards and one touchdown. He was named MVP of the game.

The game came down to a last-minute drive. That's when Rice took control. San Francisco was down 16-13 with about three minutes to go and the ball on their own eight-yard line. Quarterback Joe Montana moved his team down field like the master he was. On that drive, Rice caught three key passes including one on a crossing route where he did what he did best: run after the catch. He turned Montana's short bullet into a 27-yard gain.

Rice returned to the Super Bowl three more times after that, rising to the occasion every time. Defensive backs still have nightmares about chasing the number 80 on Rice's back. His final appearance was Super Bowl XXXVII, when he was with the Oakland Raiders. It was late in his career—he was 40 years old but still performing at a high level. Although the Raiders lost that game, Rice caught five passes including a touchdown.

PUTTING UP POINTS

Adam Vinatieri ▶

On the 49ers' first possession of Super Bowl XXIV, Jerry Rice caught a pass over the middle and was hammered by Broncos safety Dennis Smith. But the defender didn't wrap him up. Rice bounced off the hit, scanned the field ahead, and kept running all the way to the end zone.

That was only one of Rice's eight career Super Bowl touchdowns, only six of his 48 points. But in many ways it was a perfect summary of everything Rice could do. He was a student of the game, always looking to learn more. He was tough as a tree trunk but also quick. And it seemed like he was *always* turning short passes into big gains by shedding tacklers.

The second-highest scoring player in Super Bowl history is kicker Adam Vinatieri. The kicker played in five Super Bowls—four with the Patriots and one with the Indianapolis Colts. Always cool under pressure, Vinatieri booted field goals to tie or win numerous postseason games. Those include Patriots game-winners over the Rams in Super Bowl XXXVI in 2002 and over the Panthers in XXXVIII in 2004.

Other names at the top for Super Bowl points include several other 49ers. How good were the 49ers of the 1980s and 1990s? Consider this: Three of the four players tied for most points in a single Super Bowl are 49ers. That includes Rice and star running backs Roger Craig and Ricky Watters.

In Super Bowl XXIX, two 49ers scored 18 points (the single-game record): Jerry Rice and Ricky Watters. Rice is the only player to do it twice.

— MOST SUPER BOWL POINTS, — SINGLE GAME

18	Jerry Rice	49ers vs. Broncos	XXIV (3 TDs)
		49ers vs. Chargers	XXIX (3 TDs)
18	Roger Craig	49ers vs. Dolphins	XIX (3 TDs)
18	Ricky Watters	49ers vs. Chargers	XXIX (3 TDs)
18	Terrell Davis	Broncos vs. Packers	XXXII (3 TDs)

— MOST SUPER BOWL POINTS — IN A CAREER

48	Jerry Rice	49ers	4 games (8 TDs)
34	Adam Vinatieri	Patriots/Colts	5 games (7 FG, 13 PAT)
30	Emmitt Smith	Cowboys	3 games (5 TDs)

SACK MASTERS

Reggie White ▶

Many defensive linemen have a variety of techniques or "moves" they use to get to the quarterback. The swim. The spin. The rip.

The Packers' Reggie White was so strong, he didn't need many moves. He mostly just overpowered his opponents, even when being double-teamed.

White began his career in Philadelphia, where he established a reputation for being powerful *and* quick. He was stout against the run *and* a terror against the pass. When he signed with Green Bay he was older and maybe a little less quick—but still as strong as a bull.

Darnell Dockett ▼

In Super Bowl XXXI, the Patriots passed on 48 plays, compared to only 13 runs, giving White and fellow defenders plenty of chances to sack the quarterback. White set the record for sacks in a single Super Bowl. He had three, and his Packers won the game, 35-21.

That record was untouched for twelve years until Arizona's Darnell Dockett tied it in Super Bowl XLIII. Like White's Packers, Dockett's Cardinals were known mostly for their offensive stars, including quarterback Kurt Warner and wide receivers Anquan Boldin and Larry Fitzgerald. And just like when White faced the Patriots, this Super Bowl featured a lot of passing. Pittsburgh's Ben Roethlisberger dropped back 30 times, giving Dockett plenty of chances to drop him.

Dockett's three sacks were all his team got, however, and the Cards lost 23-27.

— MOST SUPER BOWL SACKS, CAREER —

4.5	Charles Haley	49ers/Cowboys	5 games
4.0	Justin Tuck	Giants	2 games
3.0	Danny Stubbs	49ers	2 games
3.0	Leonard Marshall	Giants	2 games
3.0	Jeff Wright	Bills	4 games
3.0	Reggie White	Packers	2 games
3.0	Willie McGinest	Patriots	4 games
3.0	Tedy Bruschi	Patriots	4 games
3.0	Mike Vrabel	Patriots	3 games
3.0	Darnell Dockett	Cardinals	1 game
3.0	LaMarr Woodley	Steelers	2 games

SUPER BLUES

Craig Morton ▶

The Super Bowl isn't all glory and good times. Every game has a loser, after all. And no team has lost more than the Denver Broncos, who have fallen in five of them. Several of those losses were ugly, too, like Super Bowl XII, when the Broncos lost 27-10 to the Cowboys. Or that 42-10 shellacking by Washington in Super Bowl XXII. Or the time the 49ers walked to a 55-10 victory.

— MOST SUPER BOWL — INTERCEPTIONS THROWN, CAREER

8	John Elway	Broncos	5 games
7	Craig Morton	Cowboys/Broncos	2 games
7	Jim Kelly	Bills	4 games
6	Fran Tarkenton	Vikings	3 games

But Broncos fans have reason to hold their heads high. Their team has been to eight Super Bowls (a record shared with the Cowboys, Steelers, and Patriots) and has won three of them.

The Vikings and Bills are 0–4 in the big game. The two franchises were powerhouses in different eras, but neither could take home the Lombardi Trophy. The Bills were the first to popularize the no-huddle offense. They were so good in the 1990s that they went to the Super Bowl a record four consecutive times.

It should be no surprise to see the quarterbacks of those Broncos, Bills, and Vikings at the top of another sad list: most Super Bowl interceptions. In five trips, Broncos quarterback John Elway tossed eight of them. Jim Kelly of the Bills threw seven in his four games, and Fran Tarkenton of the Vikings threw six in three games.

How about fumbles? When a player puts the ball on the ground, it seems to crush his team's spirits. By that measure, Roger Staubach of the Cowboys was one of the all-time spirit-crushers. He fumbled five times in Super Bowl games (but led his team to two championships). Jim Kelly makes an appearance on this not-so-glorious list as well. He fumbled four times in the Super Bowl.

— MOST SUPER BOWL — FUMBLES, CAREER

5	Roger Staubach	Cowboys	4 games
4	Jim Kelly	Bills	4 games
4	Kurt Warner	Rams/Cardinals	3 games
3	Franco Harris	Steelers	4 games
3	Terry Bradshaw	Steelers	4 games

TROPHY COLLECTORS

◀ *Jack Lambert*

Way back in 1933, the NFL made a few changes. It legalized the forward pass from anywhere behind the line of scrimmage and added hash marks on the field. It divided the league into two divisions and decided that the winner of each division would meet in the NFL Championship game. And it added new teams including the Pittsburgh Pirates, who later became the Steelers.

— MOST SUPER BOWL WINS —

6	Steelers	IX-X, XIII, XIV, XL, XLIII
5	49ers	XVI, XIX, XXIII, XXIV, XXIX
5	Cowboys	VI, XII, XXVII, XXVIII, XXX
4	Packers	I, II, XXXI, XLV
4	Patriots	XXXVI, XXXVIII, XXXIX, XLIX
4	Giants	XXI, XXV, XLII, XLVI

Pittsburgh didn't make it to that first ever NFL Championship game. Instead, the Western Division champion Bears defeated the Eastern Division champion Giants 23-21 at Wrigley Field in Chicago on December 17, 1933.

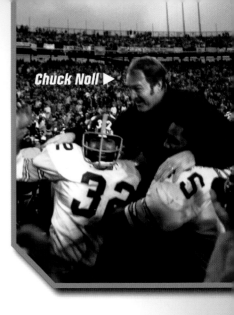
Chuck Noll ▶

The first Super Bowl was played between the champions of the AFL and NFL in 1967. In 1969 Chuck Noll took over as head coach of the Pittsburgh Steelers. The franchise still had never won a championship, but things changed under Noll. He assembled a powerhouse led by a defense nicknamed the "Steel Curtain." They won four out of six Super Bowls between 1975 and 1980. Many say that team was the best the NFL ever had.

Twenty-five years later, the Steelers became the first wild-card team in history to win three playoff road games and the Super Bowl, beating the Seattle Seahawks in Super Bowl XL. That made the Steelers the third team to win five Super Bowls. Three years later, they defeated the Arizona Cardinals in Super Bowl XLIII for their sixth title, earning a distinction no other NFL team can claim.

— MOST SUPER BOWL — VICTORIES, HEAD COACHES

Chuck Noll	Steelers	4 wins, 0 losses
Bill Belichick	Patriots	4 wins, 2 losses
Bill Walsh	49ers	3 wins, 0 losses
Joe Gibbs	Redskins	3 wins, 1 loss

GLOSSARY

draft—the process of choosing a person to join a sports team; also, to choose a person to join a sports team

dynasty—a team that is successful for a long time and wins multiple championships

immaculate—free of flaws or errors

legacy—qualities and actions that one is remembered for; something that is passed on to future generations

powerhouse—a person or team with great energy, strength, or skills.

scheme—the way a team plans and executes a play

reception——a catch of a forward pass

sack—when a defensive player tackles the opposing quarterback behind the line of scrimmage

scrimmage—in football, the imaginary line where a play begins

strategy—a careful plan or method

wild card—a team that makes the playoffs without winning its division

READ MORE

Editors of Sports Illustrated. *Sports Illustrated Super Bowl Gold: 50 Years of the Big Game.* New York: Sports Illustrated Books, an imprint of Time Inc. Books, 2015.

Frederick, Shane. *Stars of the Super Bowl.* Everything Super Bowl. North Mankato, Minn.: Capstone Press, 2017.

Rogers, Andy. *Who's Who of Pro Football.* Who's Who of Pro Sports. North Mankato, Minn.: Capstone Press, 2016.

INTERNET SITES

FactHound offers a safe, fun way to find Internet sites related to this book. All of the sites have been researched by our staff.

Here's all you do:

Visit www.facthound.com

Type in this code: 9781515726364

Check out projects, games and lots more at
www.capstonekids.com

INDEX